THE
MEDITATION
BOOK

By John Randolph Price

<u>Books</u>
*The Abundance Book

Angel Energy

The Angels Within Us

*Empowerment

Living a Life of Joy

*The Love Book

*The Meditation Book

*Practical Spirituality

*A Spiritual Philosophy for the New World

*The Success Book

*The Superbeings

*The Wellness Book

*With Wings As Eagles

*The Workbook for Self-Mastery

<u>Selected Audiocassettes</u>
*The 40-Day Prosperity Plan

*Global Mind Link/World Healing Meditation

*A Journey into the Fourth Dimension

*The Manifestation Process

*Prayer, Principles & Power

Check your bookstore for the books and audios above.
Items with asterisks can be ordered through Hay House:

800-654-5126 • 800-650-5115 (fax)

Please visit the Hay House Website at:
www.hayhouse.com

The
Meditation
Book

JOHN RANDOLPH PRICE

Hay House, Inc.
Carlsbad, CA

Library of Congress Cataloging-in-Publication Data

Price, John Randolph.
    The Meditation Book / John Randolph Price.
    p.   cm.
    ISBN 1-56170-502-0 (trade paper)
    1. Meditation.   I. Title.
BL627.P73   1998   98-3340
299' .93—dc21   CIP

ISBN 1-56170-502-0

01 00 99 98   4 3 2 1
First Printing, August 1998

Printed in Canada

"Through meditation the not-self is temporarily mingled with the Infinite, to find in this mingling the true substance of all aspiration. It is the identification of the soul with consciousness in absolute suspension. Meditation dispels the clouds which obscure the purpose of life, even as the clear rays of the sun dissipate the mist. At the climax of meditation there is the supreme moment when the unthinkable is thought, when the unknowable is known, when eternity is circumscribed with an all-sufficient mood."

— Manly P. Hall
The Phoenix

❧ CONTENTS

The Meditation Book, the fourth in a series of small volumes published by Hay House featuring a collection of my writings, focuses on the practice of meditation, which, as I pointed out in *The Superbeings*, "is the way of entering the inner Kingdom, and can be a dynamic, life-changing experience."

Let's first look at meditation from the standpoint of spiritual physics, and how it can affect not only individual beings but the world in which we live. We are told that we are the "Light of the World"—and that the Power of the Light is within us. We have also been referred to as Lightbearers and Light Beings. What does this mean? Scientists tell us that light is *energy*, producing hundreds of trillions of vibrations per second in the form of light waves. Consider now that the Source of Light is within you and that light waves are eternally emanating from your consciousness, radiating as *lines of force*. These lines of force govern electrons (the electrical charges whirling around the nucleus of atoms) and cause atoms to cluster in an energy field as a thought-form. This energy configuration is then "stepped down" through levels of substance to become visible on the physical plane.

Everything considered "matter"—whether visible or invisible—is made up of atoms, or pure energy. Therefore, everything seen and unseen is energy in motion, and this *energy of everything* is controlled by thought. The consciousness of the individual is the transmitter of energy and the directing force that destroys or creates form and experience. Contemplate this. *Destroy* means "to take away." If your health has faded, your finances dwindled, or your relationships affected adversely, you make the correction by lifting your consciousness to a higher frequency—and you do this through meditation.

The lines of force radiate from centers of High Vibration or low vibration, depending on the frequency of consciousness. You are either healing or harming—there is no in-between. You can see now why the purity of thought based on the at-one-ment principle is of vital importance. In our present world, there is much negative energy controlling the lines of force, thus creating a disruption of the natural order of things in the mineral, plant, animal, and human kingdoms.

As long as negative thought energy is the major influence on the lines of force, there will continue to be a deterioration of everything visible. And the actual renewal of all aspects of planetary life—including our personal worlds—will not begin until we reach the point where the positive exceeds the negative. At that point, when the scales are tipped in favor of constructive spiritual energy, things will begin to happen of a positive nature.

Is there any evidence that this is true? Definitely, yes! We know from scientific studies that meditation affects the first visible manifestation of organized atoms—that is, the physical body. While in meditation, the electrical activity of the brain synchronizes and brings balance and harmony to brain waves that have been out of phase and on different frequencies. The result: a higher level of intelligence and creativity. Meditation also normalizes the nervous system and causes many physiological changes that are of great benefit to the physical system.

As we move beyond the body, we see beneficial changes continuing to take place. Those individuals who regularly practice the art of meditation and have achieved a degree of spiritual consciousness find protection from, or dominion over, destructive forces and negative circumstances, and truly understand the reality of omnipresent supply, right relations, and the divine purpose in life.

There are also documented reports of group experiments with meditation resulting in substantial drops in homicides, suicides, and accidents in the test communities. And in our group meditations at Quartus, the "unified field" theory has been tested with excellent results—as evidenced by the healings in mind, body, relationships, employment, and supply.

So we see that Spirit Light not only eliminates the dark forces created by mortal mind, which are manifesting as the destructive power of nature, but also rearranges atomic substance and creates new forms and experiences for us individually. The Light within you and me is the form-building energy of all manifestation. By tuning in to the vibration of the Divine Self, and then by using our minds as radiating centers, we literally create a force field that begins to work on the etheric level to transmute negative energy and reveal the Reality that has always been behind the illusion.

It all begins with individual you and me moving through meditation into spiritual consciousness, filling our minds with spiritual energy, and thinking spiritual thoughts—all of which will activate the right lines of force. And the chain reaction of good begins in our personal lives and throughout this world.

Meditation is indeed the way to find "the true substance of all aspiration."

1

MASTERY THROUGH MEDITATION

If you've ever asked anyone to define *meditation,* you may be just as confused as you were before you asked, because it means different things to different people. My objective in this chapter is to clear up some of the confusion and discuss the practical aspects of this marvelous tool for expanding consciousness.

Meditation Benefits

Meditation will alleviate stress, reduce high blood pressure, increase resistance to disease, enhance the autonomic stability of the nervous system, improve the power of concentration, tap deep reserves of intelligence, contribute to mental clarity, stabilize emotions, improve human relations, relieve insomnia, improve coordination of mind and body, increase learning ability, and boost creativity. Numerous medical and academic studies have revealed such evidence. But of even greater importance are the *spiritual* benefits. Meditation is a tool that will enable you to make contact with your spiritual Self, and it is that intent that I will discuss first.

Definition and Use

Meditation is a relaxing of the body, a stilling of the emotions, and a narrowing of attention so that the mind may contemplate the inner Reality and move into another dimension in consciousness. There must be no effort in doing this; it must come easily and naturally. It is a gentle raising of vibrations so that one may come into alignment with the spiritual Self.

The motive for meditation must be pure, with no thought of psychic experiences or making contact with "the other side." Meditation is not an instrument for emptying the mind and creating a void to attract illusionary voices from the astral plane. To do this can be dangerous. The objective must be to establish a channel between Spirit and the lower nature, resulting in an out-pouring of the higher energy. And it is through this out-pouring that you will become receptive to the "still, small voice" from within. You will also be energized spiritually so that you will have the creative power to carry out the instructions of the Higher Self. It is important to understand that the spiritual vibration taken on during meditation becomes a positive force in the race consciousness of humanity, and is of great benefit to the animal, plant, and mineral kingdoms.

Speaking from personal experience, I have found the following guidelines to be helpful in moving from the busy world into the silence:

1.   Until you become proficient in the techniques, it is best to have several meditation periods of short duration during the day—10 to 20 minutes each.

2.   Don't take your problems with you into meditation. Remember that your primary goal is to make contact and commune with Spirit. If you take a laundry list of grievances with you, you'll never reach the secret place. And in this form of meditation, you let Spirit do the talking while you simply listen.

3. It is helpful to have a particular room and
    chair for those special times with Self, espe-
    cially during the learning/training phase. Later
    you will find that you can meditate anywhere
    at any time because the inward journey will
    have become an automatic process.

4. Begin by surrounding yourself with the
    White Light, and then commence your
    breathing exercises to relax the body and
    settle the mind and emotions.

5. Contemplate on an object or symbol *within*
    consciousness (not outside), or if you're not a
    visualizer, use a mantra. A mantra is a word
    repeated over and over again to synchronize
    the vibrations, and may be used in conjunction
    with the breathing exercises. They usually have
    no linguistic meaning, which keeps the mind
    from thinking about the significance of the
    word. If you have a favorite mantra, use it—
    otherwise, you can make one up, ensuring that
    the word has no meaning for you.

6. After a few moments of contemplating the
    symbol, the mind will shift to a spiritual idea,

which in turn will attract other divine ideas into consciousness—finally moving beyond words and into the silence. Or, in the case of the mantra, the mind will rise above the repeated impulses of the mantra and into a higher level of consciousness.

7. Once in the "upper room" of consciousness, the objective is to listen, hear, and heed the Voice within.

Over the years, Jan and I have experimented with just about every form of meditation that has come to our attention, but we had to find our own key to unlock the door to the inner Chamber, just as you will have to find yours. But perhaps we can help you in your search by sharing how we use the seven points listed above.

The Oneness Meditation

We both have a favorite chair in particular rooms where we do most of our meditating. Those chairs and rooms now have a certain vibration of energy in and around them, which makes "getting into" meditation much easier.

Second, when I sit down in the chair, I tell myself that I am now going to take time from the third-dimensional world and visit my God-Self on the Fourth Dimensional plane, and that everything on Earth can wait until I return. That sets the tone for the importance of the meditation period. Then I sit up straight, feet on the floor, hands resting comfortably in my lap, close my eyes, and surround myself with the White Light.

Next, I commence my breathing exercises, at first taking short, powerful breaths to release all tension and as a preparation for concentration. After a few minutes, I begin to focus attention on my breathing as I inhale, hold the breath, exhale, pause, and begin the cycle again. When my body is relaxed and my mind is still, I begin to concentrate on an object that I purposely call forth in my mind, such as a golden circle of light, the warm red of the rising sun, or the fire of a candle—and I begin a period of controlling my mind (thoughts) by visualizing, focusing, concentrating, and contemplating the symbol.

As I literally move into and become one with the object of contemplation, I begin to ponder my oneness with God. Sometimes a divine Truth will come forth automatically; other times the seed must be planted—a seed thought such as "I and the Father are one"—or—"Christ in me, my hope of glory." Then, as if pages are turning, other ideas or symbols are added, each revealing a truth relating to my oneness with God and my divinity, and the spiritual vibration grows stronger. After a few minutes, the "pages" become blank—the words stop—and with full alertness I move into the silence. Here I feel as one in the very presence of God. There is stillness and quiet, and my entire consciousness is in a listening mode, and it is here that the Voice speaks. It is here that the spiritual infusion is felt. It is here that the contact is made. It is here that the soul becomes an open channel for the activity of Spirit.

What I am saying will be of little benefit to you unless you experience the meditation miracle yourself, so do what you have to do to learn the techniques—then practice, practice, practice. Practice your breathing exercises. Practice focusing and concentrating on an image in your mind—or using a mantra—to control your thoughts. Practice planting seed thoughts of Truth, and watch as they give birth to higher and deeper revelations. Practice meditating on your oneness with God.

It will be well worth the effort. During and following periods of oneness with your Self, you will receive answers to your questions and guidance where there had been uncertainty. Through the contact, old error patterns will be dissolved, your consciousness will become a clear and clean center through which Spirit may work, and your world will take on new meaning as it reflects the Christ Vibration. But remember, don't try to *make* anything happen. Take the inner journey simply for the thrill of meeting your Master Self, and then let go and listen. Let go and let Spirit fulfill Itself through you.

Now let's talk about another form of meditation.

The Illusion to Reality Meditation— Also Called a "Meditative Treatment"

Whenever my consciousness gets out of tune in a particular downward direction, I try to sit down immediately and get in touch with the Reality behind the illusion. For example, let's say that you find yourself facing a financial challenge, which is outpicturing itself as limitation in your world. There is simply a misconception and a misunderstanding in your mind regarding the Source of your supply and the loving Givingness of Spirit. To meet this challenge, you should "operate" (perform spiritual surgery) on your deeper-than-conscious level of mind.

Again, you would go to your meditation place and become still, relaxed, and receptive through your breathing exercises. Then slowly and with feeling, read a Truth statement on abundance, meditating on each word and contemplating each sentence, until the true meaning registers in consciousness. Take this prosperity statement as an example:

> *The Spirit of God within me is the Source of my supply. My Christ Self knows only lavish abundance, and the activity of that Knowingness is constantly at work in my life and affairs. My Spirit is now appearing as my all-sufficiency.*

Now let's break the statement down and focus intently on the meaning and significance of the words.

The Spirit of God (contemplate the idea behind the words *the Spirit of God* until you feel something within. Speak the words silently, and watch the other thoughts that flow in to expand your thinking.)

...within me (dwell on the meaning of *within me*—what does that mean? Let the idea roll around in your mind and feeling nature until you have a degree of understanding.

...is the Source (what does *Source* mean? It means the cause, the authority, the well-spring, the foundation. Visualize a fountain of unlimited all-good within you. Get a feel for what it means to have a SOURCE of all you could possibly desire right within your consciousness.

...of my supply. (*Supply* is a word encompassing the fullness of the manifestation. It means all that you could ask for. Contemplate the idea that because your supply comes forth from an unlimited Source, then the supply itself must be unlimited.)

My Christ Self knows only lavish abundance (ponder the idea that the You of you—your Higher Self—cannot conceive of lack and limitation; therefore, there is no reality to insufficiency. There is no duality in that infinite Mind within you. It knows only all-sufficiency, abundance, copiousness, plentifulness, and surplus. And this Consciousness of Infinite Plenty is endless, limitless, boundless, and measureless.)

...and the activity of that Knowingness (contemplate the action of that Super Mind within you. Generate a greater awareness of the power at work—the force, the movement, the radiation of that All-Knowing Mind filled with thoughts of lavish abundance.)

...is constantly at work in my life and affairs. (Reflect on the word *constantly,* and gain an understanding of what it means: unfailing, permanent, enduring. Sense the divine purpose at work; feel the very Will of God, the cosmic urge to express, active in your world.)

My Spirit is now appearing as my all-sufficiency. (You are now aware of the torrent of creative-creating Energy radiating from you and going before you to manifest as the fulfillment of your desire. Think...even before the supply becomes visible, you have it. It is yours! Acknowledge this Truth with love, joy, and a heart overflowing with gratitude.)

In that state of consciousness, "wait upon the Lord." Remain still. Listen. Feel. Keep your mind focused on the Presence within, and let Spirit work in and through you with perfect ease.

Write your own meditations, and use the same procedure for wholeness in body, the healing of relationships, finding the right mate, locating a job, or any other challenge you may be facing. Just keep in mind that all you're doing in the process is opening your consciousness for the activity of Spirit. You already have everything spiritually. Your objective is simply to release it.

You can also use the "meditative treatment" approach with your favorite spiritual book. Read a line or two, meditate on the ideas behind the words until there is an inner understanding—then read a few more lines, pause for meditation, and so on. For that purpose, several specialized treatments are included in the later chapters of this book, as shown in the contents.

2

LOVE YOUR SELF: A LIVING MEDITATION

Jesus gave us the Commandment that is the first and greatest of all. He said, "Thou shalt love the Lord thy God with all thy heart, and with all thy soul, and with all thy mind, and with all thy strength." This could well be the greatest of all meditations!

The Lord *your* God is the Spirit of God within you—and you are told to love this Presence with your entire being, with everything you've got. Do you know what it means to love something totally? It means to have constant and continuous adoration for that something, to be so filled with devotion, affection, tenderness, warmth, admiration, rapture, and love toward that something that your entire consciousness is taken over by it.

Understand that when you meditate on and contemplate that Presence within—your very Spirit—with great love, that one-pointed love-focus will literally draw the awesome and incredible Power of the universe right into your thinking mind and feeling nature. You take on the Power and you become the Power and you speak as the Power—and behold—all things are made new. Your thoughts of abundance produce abundance, your feelings of wholeness produce wellness in your body, your vision of success is manifest, and your words of love bring forth the relationship you've been seeking.

When the spiritual masters of the past told us to love the true nature of our being, our Spiritual Reality, only a few people on this planet understood that this was a secret formula for health, wealth, and happiness. Only a handful interpreted it from the standpoint of practical everyday living. Only a small percentage recognized it to be the combination to the Storehouse. To love your God-Self is the greatest Commandment because within it are the secrets of the universe. And you can track this master teaching all the way back to the beginning of the Mystery Schools. It was taught by all the seers, sages, saints, and master souls of the distant past—and one of the most comprehensive teachings is found in Deuteronomy 6:5-9. We are told:

And thou shalt love the Lord thy God with all thine heart, and with all thy soul, and with all thy might. And these words, which I command thee this day, shall be in thine heart: And thou shalt teach them diligently unto thy children, and thou shalt talk of them when thou sittest in thine house, and when thou walkest by the way, and when thou liest down, and when thou risest up. And they shalt be as frontlets between thine eyes. And thou shalt write them upon the posts of thy house, and on thy gates.

Talk about dedicating your life to the love of Christ within! And when you do, your world will change dramatically. You see, when you direct your attention within through meditation, and focus that feeling of intense love toward your Higher Self, the entire vibration of your energy field is lifted up to be in tune with the Divine Vibration. And when this happens, you become a transparency for the Activity of God. The radiating Power from within will then dissolve old error patterns, false beliefs, and negative appearances, and will move through you to appear as every needed thing in your life. And the Spirit within you is so practical! If you need a better job, one will be attracted to you. If you need more money, it will come in streams of abundance. If you need a healing, the wholeness will be manifest in your body. If you need a new relationship, the right "meeting" will be arranged. You will be shown that there is the perfect supply for every demand.

Spiritual Activity

Let's take the instructions from Deuteronomy and put them into a nine-step meditative program for daily living:

Step No. 1: We are told that these words (*loving the Spirit of God within*) "shall be in thine heart." This means to impress your subconscious mind with your love of God through daily meditations—by contemplating your inner Being with all the love, adoration, and emotion you can feel. Spend time each day in "tender passion" with your God-Self.

Step No. 2: We are told that "thou shalt teach (the love of our God-Self) diligently unto thy children." Your children are your thoughts, so you begin now to train your mind —teaching it to relate only to the One Presence and Power within—and to love your Christ Self joyfully and gratefully. Whenever a negative thought enters your mind during the day, gently but firmly say, "I choose to control my thoughts by laying aside every weight and turning within to the One I love with all my heart, mind, and soul." Then think on that Inner Presence with great love.

Step No. 3: We are told to talk of our Christ Self "when thou sittest in thine house." The house is your consciousness, and to "sit" in consciousness refers to prayer or spiritual treatment. Therefore, you begin your spiritual activity by first focusing your love on the Christ within and drawing that reciprocal Love Power into your consciousness.

Step No. 4: We are told to love our Higher Self "when thou walkest by the way." This means that even in moments of idle thinking—when you are simply contemplating the activities of "this world"—you are not to forget the courtship of your True Self. The dominant trend of your thoughts must now be in this direction, regardless of what you are doing.

Step No. 5: We are told to focus that love "when thou liest down." In other words, before you go to sleep at night, again express your deep feelings of love for your beautiful Christ Self. Just say, "I love you so very much. You are so fine, so wonderful, and my love for you fills my entire being to overflowing."

Step No. 6: We are told to express that love "when thou risest up." Train yourself to begin each new day by acknowledging your Higher Self and pouring out all the love you can feel in your heart toward that Master Consciousness within. Say: "Through my love for you, I dedicate this day to you. I seek only your will, your word, your way, your work. I let my light so shine this day that I only glorify you."

Step No. 7: We are told that we shall bind this love of our Higher Self "for a sign upon thine hand." Now the hand stands for the expressing of God's ideas in the material world—and we are the channels for that expression in our daily activities. Therefore, we are told to bind—or ensure—that we make our daily work a symbol or a sign of our love of God. So do everything that is in front of you to the best of your ability, if for no other reason than for the love of your God-Self.

Step No. 8: We are told that this love for our Inner Self "be as frontlets between thine eyes." That is a direct reference to the creative imagination faculty within all of us, so words and feelings of love for your Christ Self will lift up your vision, expand your consciousness, and enable you to see with new clarity and spiritual under-standing.

Step No. 9: And finally, we are told that we shall write these words of love for our Higher Self "upon the posts of thy house, and on thy gates." In other words, keep the love of your God-Self right in the forefront of your consciousness—right within your thinking-objective mind—moment by moment, hour by hour, day by day.

These nine steps represent a living meditation, and if you make them an integral part of your daily living, your life will be forever changed. You will be a new creature—"alive with God and upheld by His free Spirit forever."

3

THE SPIRITUAL IDENTITY
MEDITATION

One of my favorite forms of healing prayer is what I call the "Spiritual Identity Meditation"—and its seed was found in Emerson's writings: "The simplest person who in his integrity worships God becomes God." This meditative prayer is based on the Fact that my real name (and yours) is...*I*. That is the name one uses when referring to personal individuality. It is also the secret word used throughout the Bible and other sacred literature to designate the individualized Presence of God, which is your true Identity. (I'm not adding the **AM** to the *I* yet; that comes later as a way of anchoring spirituality in the Earth plane.) So your proper name is none other than *I*. That *I* is the Truth of you, the Self of you, the Spirit and Soul of you. It is God being you!

Every problem that any of us could possibly have on Earth is because of an identification with our personality and not our Individuality. Accordingly, when we identify ourselves with Reality, and hold to that awareness, our consciousness of the Divine Self becomes as one—as two sides of a window pane with nothing in between to block the light.

Let us take this understanding a step further. We know that the Spirit of God cannot suffer lack, limitation, illness, or strained/broken relationships. We know that Spirit, which includes All, could never be without anything. And we know that this indwelling Master Self is never unemployed, underemployed, unfulfilled, confused, fearful, resentful, or any other characteristic attributed to the lower nature of humanhood. This Holy *I* *is* all, *knows* all, *does* all—and it is only when the little "I" gets in the way that we block the being, the knowing, and the doing. But you are not the "I." The "I" is a human creation formulated through ignorance—a mutation that exists only through false beliefs and sustained only by the power of error thinking, yet it can be redeemed by the acceptance of the *I*.

When you think, speak, or write *I*, you are not (or should not) be referring to the you who has no wisdom, no power, no vision. You are (or should be) thinking of the Master Self within—that Spirit of God as you Who is the

I-Omniscient, the *I*-Omnipotent. So the first step in training for this particular method of prayer is to meditate, contemplate, and ponder on *I* as the God-Self within.

Understand that the objective of this way of thinking and praying (meditating) is not to destroy or eliminate the personality. Rather, it is to move the lower nature into its rightful position as a witness to the Divine Activity of the *I*. We want to get to the point where the little self says, "I realize that I don't have all the answers, nor do I have the power to change my life from lack to abundance, from illness to wholeness, from discord to harmony. In fact, all the praying by humans over thousands of years has done very little for this planet and conditions in the world. So maybe it's about time to get my humanity out of the way and let my divinity take over.

"My role in the scheme of things is to simply be aware, to recognize, to be conscious of the activity of the *I* within—the activities of true place, abundance, wholeness, right relations, safety and protection, fulfillment, love, and joy. The list of good things and experiences is endless, and all that I have to do is keep my mind focused on the Master Self within, and I am kept in perfect peace."

When you transfer the thrust of your living from the little "I" to the Supreme *I*, you are also taking the burden off your shoulders and giving it to the Omnipotent Self who eliminates burdens in the twinkling of an eye. You are handing over the reins of government—the governing of your world—to the Master *I* who not only knows how to superbly administer, manage, guide, and oversee all of your affairs, but is willing to take over and do it now! After all, it's the *I*'s life we are talking about—the *I*'s body, bank account, and relationships—so don't you think that the rightful *I* should be in charge?

As your mind and emotions begin to grasp the Truth of the *I*, you will begin to understand that you do not have any problems, that you do not need anything, and that there is nothing to heal or fix or manipulate or possess. Everything just *is* right now—*is* harmonious, whole, and complete. Why? Because *I* is!

The Meditative Prayer in Four Parts

First, look within and contemplate that Magnificent *I* that you are in Truth, and begin the releasing process. Release your body, bank account, debts, relationships, job, fears, unforgiveness, uncertainties, confusion—and your past, present, and future. Surrender all to the Self who has wanted to move back into the driver's seat since the moment the ego took control. That is the beginning phase of this method of meditative prayer.

The second step is to let the Master *I* be in Earth as It is in Heaven, and you do this by adding the word **AM**. Work on this exercise for a few moments: Say to yourself silently, "I AM." Then imagine that you are hearing the Master Self within speaking the same words, *"I AM."* Usually the words as registered in the mind and feeling nature will seem to come from two different coordinates in consciousness, so your objective is to align the two **I AM**s into one voice. Keep repeating the process, silently speaking "I AM" and listening with the inner ear to Self saying *"I AM"*—and each time feel the two voices drawing closer and closer together until there is only one *I AM*.

Once you do this, you are ready for the third step, the Identity Meditation. Meditate slowly on these ideas, pausing to contemplate each line with great feeling:

> *The I AM Self in the midst of me is omnipotent, all-knowing, all-seeing, eternally doing and being.*
>
> *I know this. I feel this. I am aware of the radiating Energy of the I AM Self going before me, creating according to the Perfect Patterns, revealing the Divine Standard of wholeness, abundance, right relations, and true place fulfillment.*

Pause and feel the radiation of Divine Energy from your entire being. After a few moments, continue the meditation.

> *I am shining abundance. I am wholeness flowing into perfect expression. I AM the radiation of unconditional love. I AM the light of harmony, the beam of happiness, the ray of contentment. I AM all. All that I could ever see, I AM. Because I AM all, I HAVE all.*
>
> *Through the eyes of the I AM Self I now see the High Vision of completeness, divine order, and glorious harmony in the world. The Divine HAVE is in perfect expression.*

Pause again and see in your mind's eye—with controlled visualization—everything as perfect in your life. Feel with your emotions what you are seeing: a Life Experience of total joy, love, beauty, abundance, wholeness, harmony, creativity, an easy flow of accomplishment, great peace, and contentment. Keep watching the *controlled* mental movie until you are completely satisfied that every activity in your life is in divine order—then expand your vision to see people throughout the world enjoying a Life Experience as fulfilling as yours. Then return to the meditation.

*I have seen the Truth. My affairs are now
an extension of the I AM Self, an expression of
my Divine Consciousness. Because I HAVE all,
there is nothing more to seek. I now live as the
I THAT I AM. I have moved from an attitude of
becoming to a Consciousness of Being. I now
rest in my Beingness.*

Be still and rest now in the Presence of your Holy
Self, listening to the inner Voice. From the moment the
meditation is concluded, you move into the fourth step,
which is to live your life as a prayer. To look into someone's eyes and behold the *I* is a prayer. To silently com-
municate with Nature, recognizing the *I* in all, is a
prayer. To forgive all is a prayer. Gratitude is a prayer.
Sharing is a prayer. Everything you do should be a
prayer—and continuously flowing through your mind
are the words, "The *I* is doing and being everything
now; I cannot want for anything."

You live the prayer and the prayer lives you, and
taking thought for tomorrow is replaced by living in
the joyful now.

4

MEDITATIVE TEACHINGS FROM THE MASTER WITHIN

The focus of this chapter is to channel the teachings of your Master Self, the idea being to meditate on the Presence within, and then listening and writing down what you hear. If there are only feelings and symbols at first, ask yourself, "What do I intuitively feel that Spirit is saying to me?"—and write what comes into your mind. Meditate, listen, write. Meditate, listen, write. The "lessons" received will deal with ways to deepen the realization of the Presence, how to co-create with Spirit to move beyond a challenge, ideas to make your spiritual work more effective, weaknesses in consciousness that must be strengthened, glimpses of the future, dream interpretations, and on and on.

I have found it helpful to go into a period of deep, relaxed meditation and speak the following: "Beloved Christ within, the Living God of my being, I humbly invite you to think through me now. I won't try to stop my own thinking, nor will I try to think specific thoughts. I'll simply let go and let You speak into my mind." And then affirm: "The Christ Presence is now using my mind to think, and I am totally receptive to the Word."

Usually I will speak this statement aloud three times, and then silently three times, which shifts my consciousness into the listening mode. As the thoughts begin to come through, they are transcribed on paper— and then I spend time studying and meditating on the lessons for deeper realizations of truth.

Another method of tuning into the Higher Consciousness is to meditate for a time, then while you are still in that deeply relaxed but alert state, let your imagination take you into the forest or to a mountain. There, meet someone who in your mind represents divine wisdom and understanding. Perhaps it's a kindly old man with white hair who beckons you to come sit beside him. Greet this image with great honor and respect, and look into his eyes immediately. You may ask his name if you like, and he will surely respond. When you feel comfortable with your friend, begin to ask your questions. Move into a relaxed give-and-take dialogue, as if in an informal interview with a Master Soul. In *Practical Spirituality,* I wrote about my imaginary meeting on the cliff with Asher. This wise old man represented the Master Energy of my Higher Self giving me a view of the world and a look at the future.

The first intuitive message that I attributed to Spirit came forth in 1967, and ten years later I heard the first audible words. During those years and continuing to this day, I've received enough messages to fill several books. In fact, my books are, for the most part, the result of communications from within—colored of course by my own particular energy and conditioned to the degree of my realization of Truth. A few examples follow, given to you to stimulate your own process of meditating, listening, and writing—to produce your own textbook of meditative teachings from the Master within.

> *You say that you have faith in God, that you believe in God, that you trust God. But I ask you, how can you believe in God and profess faith and trust if you do not know me? Yes, I am closer than your very breath, but what meaning does that have for you?*
>
> *If you were attempting to be friendly to a new neighbor, or were establishing a relationship with an acquaintance, would you not take the time to get to know the individual? Your first*

consideration would be one of courtesy, kindness, and respect. If the neighbor or the acquaintance knocked at your door, your response would be to welcome the person and express hospitality. You would talk, share, and listen together. Yet when I knock at the door of your consciousness, ready to provide you with the Word and the Way, I am usually ignored.

You do not talk to me, nor do you listen to me. It is as if I did not exist...until there is a problem. Can you not understand that I am alive, that I live, that I am a living being? I think, I see, I speak, I listen, I know, I love. Am I not worthy to be acknowledged, at least in the measure of a neighbor or an acquaintance? Am I not at least as important as your troubles? Then why do you think more about your troubles than you do of me?

You cannot say that you have not had the benefit of my presence, because I know that you have felt the feeling of love in your heart. You cannot say that you have not seen me, because I appear as Light to the inner eye and an overshadowing presence to your mind. You cannot say that you have not heard me, for I am forever speaking through your intuition and whispering thoughts into your mind.

Who am I? What is there in a name, a word, or a title? I wear many faces. Some call me the Christ. To others I am God. I am also referred to as the Father, the Son, the Holy Spirit, the Monad, Atma, Buddi, Higher Mind, Soul, Self. I am all that you once were and can be again. I am the Purity of you, the Reality of you, the Life of you, the Essence of you, the Love of you, the Person of you. To the personality of the lower self, I am a friend, guide, teacher, perfector of concerns, freer of burdens, healer of ills, filler of lacks, and harmonizer of conditions. Even more, I am the cause, creator, source—and the effect, the creation, the result. Understand this.

Where am I? I am around, in, and through you. You live, move and have your being in me, and I in you. When you sit, I sit with you. When you walk, I walk with you. I am where you are—eternally.

It is dawning on you now, as you think of the who and the where of me, that I am You—the You not caught in the web of the illusion, the You of a higher dimension. Do you see me? I exist simultaneously in all dimensions, all planes, all frequencies and vibrations. I am pure Light, yet my radiance dims on the lower plane of consciousness. I am the Cosmic Fire, yet my flame is but a flicker in the depths of mortal mind. I am the Music of the Spheres, yet my harmony rings unmelodious in the world of materiality.

Now do you see me? Do you see You? There is but One...there is no "we"...there is only I. From the highest of the above to the lowest of the below, there is only I.

When I say talk to me, listen to me, the "me" is not something separate from you. It is the inner you, the deeper you, the higher you, the holy you. Can you not talk to your Self, listen to your Self, and love your Self?

I am your Truth. Know me and be free.

❦ ❦ ❦

Dismiss all thoughts of right and wrong, for in truth, you have done neither. Every action you have ever taken was as a child running home in the darkness of night. If you stumbled, it was because you could not see. If you fell, it was your loss of balance. Why call it right or wrong? Set a clock to a certain time and wind it up. The mechanism is running, the clock is ticking. Unless the hands are changed, the clock will proceed on a definite course. Your consciousness is like the clock. Unless it is changed, it will continue as is. Once set, it is in action; and everything it feels, thinks, says, or does is dictated by its beliefs. Are they right? Are they wrong? That is not the point. The point is, you cannot act contrary to your consciousness. You cannot express any differently than you are in consciousness. Understand this, and forgiveness toward all will not be difficult.

❦   ❦   ❦

Consider a challenge as a choice, a choice made by you to reinforce your I AM—to realize that I AM the answer, the solution. I am the I AM. I am Omnipotence, and nothing can stand against me, and remember that I am you. This You that I AM is a present help in every difficulty, seeking only to move through your consciousness and touch the unreal appearance— and it is no more. In its place is the reality of harmony. Can you not trust me? Will you not let me be responsible for that which concerns you?

You chose the challenge to prove me, yet when the test appeared, you forgot me. You staged the performance and cast me as the hero, as the deliverer and producer of miracles, yet when the play began, I was left out of the script—replaced by you and your mortal sense of stress and strain. Without me, the challenge cannot be met...it can only be replaced with another challenge. With me, only the good is triumphant. I AM always victorious in every situation. Trust me!

❦ ❦ ❦

There is something between me and your phenomenal world. It is your consciousness. Your world mirrors that which is closest to it; therefore, your world is reflecting your consciousness. If you would have your world reflect my nature of loving sufficiency, I must be brought in to your consciousness—even to the outer rim, so to speak. There I stand before your world, and the Truth is revealed. No good thing is then withheld from you. But you must not direct or prescribe the way. I am the way. Leave it in my hands. Be as a little child in joyful anticipation, keeping your thoughts on me, caring not and trusting me, fearing not and loving me.

❦ ❦ ❦

Yes, I keep my promises. I even had my assurances put in writing in passages of the Bible and in other sacred works. This was my contract with you, which did not require your signature to go into effect, for my promises are Law. Your only responsibility is to acknowledge that I exist and to believe what I said. It is as simple as that.

I have said, as it is written, that I will bring all the good that I promised, and I have promised much. I have said that you can call upon me in the day of trouble and I will deliver you, and I emphasized my love for you by saying that even before you call, I will answer.

I have said that you must not fear, for I am with you, that in my presence is fullness of joy. I have asked that you trust me with all your heart, and lean not on your own understanding. Do you see the significance of this? It is MY understanding that pierces the illusion, not yours. It is MY power that removes the difficulty, not yours. Trust me. Lean on me.

Until you transcend the ego, you can do nothing but add to the insanity of the world. That statement should delight you rather than create despair, for it removes the burdens from your shoulders. While you learn and grow and let your consciousness unfold, I will do the work for you, through you, as you. But I must have your total attention. This is what I meant when I said that by acknowledging me in all your ways, I would direct your paths.

I have promised you strange and wonderful things, if only you would place your faith in me and not in the outer world. I have said that I go before you to level the mountains, to harmonize anything that may concern you, and that I would perform that which is yours to do. Could I make it any plainer?

I have promised you unlimited prosperity, and contrary to your belief, I have not imposed any conditions. I give freely to saint and sinner; it is your consciousness that imposes the limitations. But I have told you how to surmount this obstacle.

As it is written, you are told that as long as you seek me, you are made to prosper. The seeking is the key, for you cannot fully focus on the outer world of limitations while searching for me and my Kingdom within.

You have also been told that the meek shall possess the land and delight themselves in abundant prosperity. Do you know what meek *means? It comes from an ancient word depicting that which is unresistant, easily molded. Look again at what I said: Those who do not resist their good and who consent to have their consciousness molded by me shall possess the land and delight themselves in abundant prosperity.*

As it is written, I have opened unto you my treasure, ensuring that you always have an all-sufficiency in all things. And when I said to simply love me and you would have peace within your walls and prosperity within your palaces, I was giving you the secret of the Law of Attraction. To love me with all of your being is to draw forth my Kingdom into your consciousness, and the fullness of my abundance is made evident in your world.

I have promised you wholeness, saying, as it is written, that I am the Lord your healer; that I heal all your diseases; restore health to you; and heal your wounds. This is not to come, It is. In truth, you are healed now...you are whole.

To those who revere my name, the sun of righteousness shall rise with healing in its wings. Think on this and see the simple instructions. A single eye on the Holy Self within receives Light into consciousness, revealing the absence of disease and the already present reality of wholeness. I am the Fountain of Healing Life. Will you not drink freely of me?

I have promised you protection. As it is written, when you pass through the waters, I will be with you, and the rivers will not over-flow you, and when you walk through fire, you will not be burned. Even if a host of enemies should encamp against you, you will not fear, for I will hide you. Stay close to me, and let my shield shine through your consciousness to form a ring-pass-not.

Is anything too hard for me? No. And who am I? I am You. Not the human you, but the Spiritual You, the Master You, the one called a priest after the order of Melchizedek. One day soon you will awaken, and my Consciousness will be yours and nothing shall be impossible to you. He who comes to you then shall never hunger, and he who believes in you shall never thirst, and he who follows you shall not walk in darkness. For I will be You and You will be Me, eternally the one and only Reality.

I keep my promises.

Now begin your own book of meditative teachings from within. Meditate, listen, write. Meditate, listen, write.

5

MEDITATIVE TREATMENTS FOR ONENESS WITH SPIRIT

Do your preparatory work, then read each meditation slowly, pondering the ideas, contemplating the words, absorbing the meaning behind the words, and feeling the truth in your heart. Remember, you are changing your belief system, moving from false ideas to a higher plane in consciousness where glorious Reality exists in all its fullness.

Spirit of the living God within, my Spirit, my very God-Self...my heart overflows with love for you. My Soul sings songs of boundless adoration for you...my mind reaches out to you in total devotion...and I radiate the love I am and have to you with all the power of my being. Oh, I love you so much! You are all I seek, and nothing in my life is more important than my oneness with you.

You are my beloved Self, and when I look within and feel and see and know you, I am beholding the Truth of all. Every person who has ever been a part of my consciousness is in Reality none other than you. I understand this, and now I can love everyone as my Self, for I see my Self in all, as all. My relationships of the past, present, and future are now enfolded in love and harmonized for the good of all.

It is so wonderful to realize that there is but one Self, one Presence, one Power. Thank you, my glorious Spirit Self, for this understanding. And thank you for understanding me...for knowing every detail of my life...for seeing not only my needs, but also the fulfillment of those needs. God knows! And because you know, the questions are already answered, the problems are already solved, for Divine action eternally follows Divine Knowingness.

Now I can relax and behold the Activity of God, knowing that it is the only Power at work *in my life and affairs. The dynamic movement of Creative Energy is taking place now, in and through me. My Spirit knows exactly what to do, and is doing it now. The crooked places have been straightened, and that which concerns me has been perfected. The earthly illusion has been replaced with the Heavenly Vision; and I am now whole, strong, and free.*

❧ ❧ ❧

God is right where I am, and I am eternally aware of this Presence. God conceived within Its Mind an Idea of Itself in expression. I am that Idea made manifest. God is expressing as me now. I am the expression of God. I am the Christ.

The Law, the creative energy of God-Mind, is flowing through the Idea that I am now living. That Idea is the Christ, the Self-expression of God that I am, and my world becomes a reflection of that Idea.

As Christ is the Healing Principle, so the Law restores my body according to the Perfect Pattern.

As Christ is the Abundance Principle, an all-sufficiency of supply now manifests for my use.

As Christ is the Harmony Principle, all of

my relationships are lovingly renewed and strengthened.

I am now the Living Truth of Wholeness and Fulfillment.

❧   ❧   ❧

I am invisible, for Spirit is invisible and I am Spirit.

I am invisible, for Cause is invisible and I am Cause.

I am invisible, for Soul is invisible and I am Soul.

I am invisible, for Consciousness is invisible and I am Consciousness.

I am invisible, for Body is invisible and I am Body.

I am invisible; therefore, in prayer and meditation I seek that which is invisible, for to seek form is contrary to my nature.

I am invisible; therefore, my supply is invisible, for it is substance, the pure essence of my Consciousness.

I am invisible, and to judge that which is seen is to decree lack and limitation, for what is seen is but an infinitesimal fragment of that which infinity is.

I am invisible, and so is my love, wisdom, power, health, abundance, peace, harmony, joy, and the essence of my relationships.

I am invisible. As my consciousness of the invisible Activity of Spirit expands, the greater and grander will be the manifestations in my life, for the invisible Cause is infinite and the forms eternally unlimited, yet that which is seen in mind as finite is forever limited in visible expression.

I am invisible.

❧   ❧   ❧

I listened for the eagle, and I heard the call to commence the journey Home. The instruction was so simple, yet the rewards so great: "They that wait upon the Lord shall renew their strength; they shall mount up with wings as eagles; they shall run, and not be weary; and they shall walk, and not faint.

I am now dedicating my life to the Living Christ within, and I am indeed strong. My youth is renewed like the eagle's, and I have risen from my sickbed and now stand forth with vigor and power, knowing only the Life Force of Wholeness. I am lifted above deprivation and scarcity, and I am soaring in the limitless sub-stance of abundance. I am protected under the shadow of the Almighty, and no evil can befall me. I am set on high, on a rock, above all sor-row and anguish. And my heart has been opened to love, a love so great, so uncondition-al, that it has attracted to me heaven's bound-less measure of adoration.

I have given up the little self for the Holy Self, and I have found the Way. I have wings as eagles, and into the heavens I have flown, a flight of joy and gladness that has taken me to the Secret Place on the Mountain, the very Kingdom of God. And here I run, and I am not weary; and I walk, and I do not faint.

The Dawn is here. The Eagles are flying.

6

MEDITATIONS FOR CLEANSING ERROR PATTERNS

A ll disharmony in life is caused by false beliefs that we have entertained in consciousness, which formed error patterns that were projected into the outer world of form and experience. Let's begin now to burn away the residue of the old belief system—our ego thoughts—through cleansing meditations. Remember, we want our world to be a perfect reflection of the Reality within.

✣   ✣   ✣

I enter the chamber of my consciousness and look deeply within. I examine all the thoughts, feelings, and beliefs that have been stored there for so long. As each error thought appears, I release it to the indwelling Christ and let it go.

There are those I know well should be eliminated, and then there are those that are hidden, buried deeply, for I could not quite face them. Even now I hesitate to expose them for fear of the pain that they may bring, or changes I may not want to accept. Yet I have the urge to move up higher, and I cannot take them with me. I will ask the Presence to go before me and lead the way.

Divine Love, please show me the barriers that hold me from my oneness with you, my beautiful Christ Self. Let your Light dissolve, even as it reveals the errors in my consciousness. Dear God, who art within me, I am willing to surrender all that I am to you. Show me the way. I cannot do it alone. Lift me up, my Spirit, to your Consciousness, that I may see the Light and be made new and whole and free.

If I hold any one of your children in condemnation or unforgiveness, I choose to release them. I choose to give to all whom I feel obligated their due. I love them. I bless them. I wish them their highest good. I choose to withhold *from no one what is theirs. I choose the very highest of your Good for all.*

Show me the way to surrender my life, my body, my love, my mind, my family, my debts, my fears, my possessions, my thoughts, words, and deeds to the Higher Self within. If I must let something go, take it. If I must do something, show me, tell me, direct me. Take me as I am, and lift me up to your highest Vision. I hold back nothing. If I do, show me and I will hold it back no longer.

I choose to surrender. I choose to understand. I choose to believe in you and nothing else and show forth only your fruits in my experience.

At this moment, I am lifted up into the Christ Consciousness where there is only Light and Love and Life.

❧   ❧   ❧

I agree from this moment on to do my very best to keep my mind on the Presence within, to feel love and joy, to think loving thoughts toward all, and to always act from a sense of inward direction.

To accomplish this, I now release all fears, concerns, resentment, condemnation, and unforgiveness. I surrender all past mistakes and errors in judgment, and I empty out all false pride and ego-centered emotions.

Everything in my consciousness that could possibly hold me in bondage I now cast upon the Christ within to be dissolved. I now choose to live under grace, to be the perfect open channel through which Divine Love, Wisdom, and Power flow forth as the Activity of Spirit in my life. And I see and know this Activity to be the perfect harmonizing of all relationships, the perfect adjustment in all situations, the perfect release from all entanglements, the perfect supply for abundant living, the perfect health of my body, and the perfect fulfillment in my life.

I now go forth in faith, putting my trust in the Christ within, and living each moment with a heart overflowing with gratitude, love, and joy.

❧   ❧   ❧

I was created as a Supreme Expression of Supreme Being. I did not create myself. God extended Itself and expressed Itself as the

Individual Being I AM. Therefore, all that God is, I AM. I AM one whole Being—a thinking, knowing, understanding, loving, omnipotent Self endowed with the free gift of God's will to continue the creative process of all that is good, true, and beautiful.

If my circle of life does not reflect this Truth of wholeness and harmony, it is because of an interlocking chain of beliefs, the sum-total of which form the self-created ego. The ego is the idea that I made up about myself; it is my image of myself. The energy of these ego beliefs blocks the natural flow of spiritual ener-gy into matter, but I do not have to continue believing these beliefs. I can change my mind, and I choose to do so beginning now.

My mind is the agent of the Master Self within. It is an extension of the Light from on High, and therefore my mind is powerfully creative. Everything that is not perfect in my life is a manifestation of false beliefs in my mind, and all false beliefs are related to fear. What I am afraid of produces false beliefs. What am I afraid of? Regardless of my answer, it is the subconscious fear that I am more pow-erful than God.

*My evidence of this is my body, my rela-
tionships, my financial affairs, and the overall
condition of my life. God does not cause, will,
or authorize sickness, discord, lack, or unful-
fillment; yet I have experienced these things,
which led to the apprehension that I have the
power to countermand the Divine Principles. I
became afraid of my power, and therefore I
chose to be weak to restore power to God. The
root fear that I can override God's will has also
resulted in a parent belief that says, "The world
of effects with which I identify has more power
than God." And the outcroppings of this belief
have multiplied into a family of false beliefs.*

*The first step out of this quagmire is to say
to myself with passionate feeling: **"I choose
not to believe falsely, because there is nothing
beneficial in such beliefs."** I had chosen to
believe these thoughts; therefore, it was the
thoughts in my mind that produced the disharmony and not the effects of my world, for effects
are not cause. My insufficiency is not connect-
ed at all to any economic situation. My physical ailments are never related to my body. The
problem in any relationship has nothing to do
with another person. My disappointments and*

failures in my work are far removed from the economy, my employer, or other people in the workplace. By understanding this and placing the responsibility where it belongs, I realize that no one has ever done anything to me. It was all the error thoughts in my mind being outpictured.

The second step out of this madness is to call in the cold Fire of Spirit to burn away all residue of my former system of false beliefs and error patterns. I do that now with deep, passionate feeling.

Spirit of the Living Fire, pour Thyself on me that I may be consumed in the flames of purification. I cast all beliefs into the all-consuming fire; I let all error thoughts burn in the purifying fire; I let my judging emotions pass away in the loving fire; I find my freedom in the cleansing fire; I see myself healed in the invisible fire. I rest in the Living Fire, and I become the Spiritual Fire.

The third step in my escape from prison is to withdraw all resentment toward anyone or anything in the outer world. No one, no thing, has ever done anything to me, so I pull back all projections of ill will, hurt feelings, and irrita-

*tion. This is what it means to forgive. And I for-
give myself by withdrawing all displeasure with
myself, knowing that under ego influence I simply made the mistake of believing in something
that was not real. But I have changed my mind.*

*And the fourth step toward freedom is to
look up to Truth, to reconnect with the Light in
consciousness and accept the radiation of
Divine Love flowing from above—and to think
thoughts based only on the Principle of Truth.
My commitment now is to use my mind as a
channel for the Master Self I AM, as it was at
the beginning of creation.*

And the creation begins anew this day.

※   ※   ※

Once error patterns are dissolved, Divine Order
takes place. When you experience Divine Order, your
life is in balance, with a distinct feeling of equilibrium and symmetry. There is a sense of rhythm, as
being in a natural flow. There is harmony as you find
yourself filled with peace, contentment, and a unity
with all life.

Follow your cleansing meditation with the short,
powerful decrees shown below—all with a feeling of joy.

I AM a radiating center of total peace.
I AM the harmony that will never cease.
I AM the power to do, to have, to be.
I AM the life that is eternally free.
I AM the way, the truth, the light.
I AM an eagle in preparation for flight.

Pause a moment to feel the power building in your consciousness, then say:

In the name and through the power of the Presence I AM,
I now decree Divine Order in my life and affairs.
Let the abundance I AM be revealed.
Let the wholeness I AM be manifest.
Let the love I AM be expressed.
Let the Will of God be done!

7

MEDITATIVE TREATMENTS FOR REALIZING TRUE WORTH

Pause for a moment, and feel and see with your mind's eye the infinite Ocean of God-Energy that is everywhere present at once. At the very center of this omnipresent Creative Energy, see a circle of light. This circle represents *you* as a conscious Being, infinite Spirit individualized. Recognize that the Light, Force, Power, Energy, Substance, Life—both outside and inside the circle—are identical. There is no separation, nothing is divided, all is the same. The circle of light simply represents the Infinite being aware of Itself at a point of Self-Awareness. Therefore, *your* very existence, *your* essence, *your* life force, *your* energy, is one and the same as the Infinite Presence of God.

We have the Cause of all things within us. The Divine Consciousness of our Self is eternally causing all things. What we are seeing in our phenomenal world is how our low-worth consciousness limits the Causing of Spirit. To stop limiting the Unlimited, we must embody the Truth of Who and What we are—our *True* Worth. And in this consciousness we can say without the slightest reservation...*without me, God would not be complete...without me, the universe would lose its equilibrium.* Let's move up to that altitude of mind.

❧   ❧   ❧

I understand my true worth now. I had thought that I was a human being with a mortal mind subject to the trials and tribulations of this world. All of that is in the past, for I have come to my Self and have recognized that Self as the only Reality. And as the I AM THAT I AM, I could not ask for more than I already have. My worth is infinite, for I AM in truth, the Worthiness of God.

How could I not love and adore such Magnificent Completeness? I love my wholeness with all my heart, with all my soul, with all my mind, with all my strength. I know that to love my God-Self is the greatest commandment because it is the greatest secret. It is the Law of Attraction, the very Will of God that brings and holds everything together for good. And so I pour in that love to my precious Self, and the reciprocal action of my Self flows out as Unconditional Love, becoming its own channel to attract and receive the highest form of Good in the Universe.

I now go forward as the instrument for the Creative Expression of God. I now let the Magnificent Spirit I AM fulfill Itself on Earth as me.

❦   ❦   ❦

I came into this world with a very specific purpose.

I came to fulfill a mission.

I came to love life and realize the truth about me.

I came to contribute to the salvation of this world.

I am a part of God and fullness of the Godhead dwells in me. In the Mind of God, no one, or no thing, is useless or meaningless. Everyone and everything is of critical importance to the balance and order of the universe.

Without me, God would not be complete.

Without me, the universe would lose its equilibrium.

All that is before me to do, I do with happy enthusiasm.

For nothing is too insignificant.

And never again will there be a sense of futility in my life. I am overflowing with gratitude to the Father for the opportunity to be in physical form at this time.

I am so thankful to be right where I am, right now, serving all who come my way with love, joy, understanding, and forgiveness.

Recognizing my true worth, I now go forth with uplifted vision. I see with the inner eye the loving and prospering activity of the Christ within.

I see with my physical eyes lavish abundance everywhere.

I am peaceful, powerful, and poised, for I know who I am.

8

MEDITATIONS FOR PHYSICAL AND FINANCIAL WELL-BEING

Physical Wellness

Ideas such as sickness, disease, and old age do not exist in the Mind of God. Therefore, as the pure Energy of God-Mind expresses as the Life Principle and forms the body according to the Perfect Pattern, the visible manifestation must also be perfect. Since we were created out of perfection, we must be perfect. But how do we explain the appearance of disease and sickness? Go back to the principle that in the Mind of God, thoughts are creative, and since we are individualizations of God, our thoughts are also creative. We have the freedom to create conditions and experiences in our lives according to the thoughts we think and accept as true. Thus, we create our own diseases by objectifying fear, hate, worry, or other mental-emotional disturbances. But we can also be restored to our normal state of perfection through the right use of our minds.

Any idea that is registered as a conviction in our deeper mind results in a change in our world, beginning with the body. When we begin to consider that the healing principle within is the Cause of our physical well-being, the negative energy within our individual force field begins to change. In other words, physical perfection is the natural state of our being, and as this Truth is accepted in our thinking and feeling natures, our bodies will change accordingly. So a "healing" is simply a return to our natural state.

Let's accept the Truth of our Being through meditation. The meditations in chapter 5, contemplating the Oneness with Spirit, are excellent for this purpose, with the treatments shown below used as daily meditative reminders.

❦   ❦   ❦

The Spirit of God is the Life Force within me; and every cell of my body is filled with the intelligence, love, and radiant energy of God-Mind.

God's will for me is perfect health, and God sees me as perfect; therefore, wellness is the natural state of my being.

Ideas such as sickness, disease, and old age cannot exist in the Mind of God. That Mind is my mind, so I now see myself as God sees me...strong, vital, perfect.

I am now lifted up into the Consciousness of Wholeness. I accept my healing. I am healed now! And it is so.

✻ ✻ ✻

The forgiving, cleansing love of Christ now frees me from every negative thought and emotion. I now turn within and open the door to the River of Life and let the healing currents flow through me.

I am purified and vitalized by this Christ Life within. I am renewed according to the perfect pattern of Spirit.

God sees me as well, whole, complete, vibrant, strong, and perfect. And so I am!

✻ ✻ ✻

It is important to remember that following each meditative treatment, you must *be* health—which means *living* the meditation throughout the day. You totally identify with the Wholeness you are and take the idea of Absolute Well-Being and become it. You "soak" yourself with the idea from top to bottom, inside and out, day in and day out. You let the dynamic energy of Wholeness saturate your mind and animate your feeling nature, and you continuously live and move and have your being in this invigorating and nourishing force field of radiant perfection.

You breathe only wellness; you think only perfect health; you feel only hardihood; you speak only words of completeness. You *live* health...you live your natural state of being eagerly, enthusiastically, vigorously. You stay poised and confident, detached from all appearances of sickness and disease in the world, keeping your mind in tune with the spiritual understanding of Absolute Wholeness radiating from your Perfect Self.

❦   ❦   ❦

(For further readings on health and wholeness, see *The Wellness Book,* published by Hay House, Inc.)

Financial Wholeness

Do you want more money, more prosperity in your life? Then shift from a consciousness of effects (materiality) to a consciousness of cause (spirituality). When you give power to an effect, you are giving it *your* power. You are actually giving the effect power over you. Does money have power? If you say yes, you have given it your power and you have become the servant. You have reversed the roles.

Turn within and watch the Inner Presence work. The activity of your Infinite Mind sees and knows only abundance—and in this sea of Knowingness is a spiritual Idea corresponding to every single form, event, circumstance, condition, or experience that you could possibly desire. The creative energy of these Divine Ideas is forever flowing into perfect manifestation. But remember, if you constantly look to the effect, the visible form, you will create a mutation, a less-than-perfect manifestation. By keeping your focus on Spirit, however, you will keep the channel open for the externalization of Spirit according to the Divine Idea.

The time must come when you will satisfy a need for money by steadfastly depending on the Master Self within and not on anything in the outer world of form. Until you do this, you will continue to experience the uncertainties of supply. You must learn this lesson, and until you do, you will be given opportunity after opportunity in the form of apparent lack and limitation.

You may be experiencing such a challenge right at this moment. Realize that this is the opportunity you have been waiting for to demonstrate the Truth of your birthright. Know that this entire experience is but an illusion, an outpicturing of your beliefs, an effect of your consciousness. But you are going to stop giving any power to the illusion, the effect. You are going to cease feeding it with negative energy. You are going to focus only on the lavish abundance of divine substance—the very Love of God—that is forever flowing from that Master Consciousness within you. Take your stand, and prove God now!

❦   ❦   ❦

My purpose as a personality is to be consciously aware of the Divine Consciousness within, the Holy Master Self I AM in Truth. In the silence and stillness of my being, I am now aware of this Blessed Sacredness, and I feel the Presence flooding me with Light.

This Great Self I AM is being, doing, and having everything now through my recognition of Its glorious Being. So this day I give up trying to make something happen, and I place my total dependence on the Reality within. I trust this Master Self, and I am kept in perfect peace as I keep my mind stayed on the God-Being I AM.

Through my recognition of the only Cause and the only Source within, I become in tune with the Higher Law of Abundance. I am now conscious of the Inner Presence as my Supply. My consciousness of God as my abundance is my abundance, and with this understanding my consciousness becomes the law of abundance unto me. I understand. I know.

I feel alive all over and energetic throughout my being. I am vitally alert and wonderfully imaginative. I am highly stimulated and totally motivated, and I work with divine inspiration to be a clear and clean channel for the Creative Force pouring through me.

I feel this dynamic flow of Energy, and I love what I feel. The radiation is warm and sensuous. There is a deep, mutual love and attraction as this bright golden substance, the creative thread of the Universe, moves easily and effortlessly through the eye of the needle I am, weaving the rich fabric of my life. It goes before me to reveal the reality of continuous abundance and prosperity everywhere present.

I rise above the level of the lower nature now and look below. I recognize what appear to be needs on the third dimensional plane, and I acknowledge that those needs are now being fulfilled by the Activity of Spirit. That which I

AM and HAVE is coming forth into visibility in the phenomenal world.

I see it happening. The streams of Creative Energy are flowing mightily, flooding my life and affairs with abundance. The Light of God has completely illumined my world, and the darkness of lack and limitation has been dispelled. I see this clearly with my inner vision. And I behold this invisible Essence coming forth into visibility now and being attracted to the Magnetic Center I AM.

The Energy of Love has manifested as money and every other good thing, and all that I could need or want is rushing to me now. Everything that I see is Spirit made manifest, energy in form; therefore, everything is spiritual. And I accept all the Good in the name of I AM, for the fullness of all belongs to the Master Self within. Now every question is answered, every problem solved, every need fulfilled...as it was in the beginning.

(For the 40-Day Prosperity Plan and Meditation, please refer to *The Abundance Book*, published by Hay House, Inc.)

9

MEDITATION FOR TOTAL FULFILLMENT

What is fulfillment? It is completion, the crowning achievement, the "finishing touch." It is delight, happiness, and total contentment. Isn't that what we're all striving for? Let's find that *divine* fulfillment through this meditation.

❧   ❧   ❧

What do I know of God? God is Life, Life is omnipresent, all is alive. I see this in the wonders of nature. I see this in myself. I am alive because I am Life. My Life is God's Life. My Life is God. I feel my livingness within me. I feel God. My awareness of God is growing.

God is Love. I feel Love in my heart and know that this is the very Spirit of God flowing through my feeling nature. I could not love without God. I love; therefore, I am one with God. My understanding of God is growing.

Where is God? God is where I AM. God is what I AM. I AM an individualization of God, and the Spirit of God dwells within me, as me. I AM the Light of the world. I turn within to the Light and say, "Thou art the Christ, the Spirit of the Living God. You are my Spirit, my Soul, my Body. When I look at Thee, I see Me." And I listen in the Silence for the acknowledgment from within.

I am now conscious of God, of my Christ Self. I AM the Christ of God, the Truth of God, the Self of God. Through this consciousness of the Reality of me, I open the door to Spirit. I draw into my mind and feeling nature the Wholeness of Spirit, the Allness of God, and my consciousness is filled with the Light of Truth.

I know now that there is nothing that I could truly desire that is not at this very moment standing at the door of my conscious-ness, ready to appear in my life and affairs. I have only to be conscious of this Truth, and every need is met, every problem solved, every question answered. My consciousness of God within is all I will ever need for all eternity.

What is God?

God is Lavish Abundance.

I am now conscious of God within as my abundant supply.

God is Perfection, total Wellness.

I am now conscious of God within as my radiant health.

God is Perfect Love.

I am now conscious of God within as the activity of my loving relationships.

God is Perfect Harmony.

I am now conscious of God within as the harmony of my home and business.

God is the only Power.

I am now conscious of God within as my safety and protection.

God is the only Presence.

I am now conscious of God within as the guiding, guarding, protecting Presence watching over my loved ones.

God is Perfect Peace.

I am now conscious of God within as total peace on Earth.

My consciousness of God within as each of these experiences is the experience in my life and affairs. I am now experiencing only God in mind and manifestation.

My consciousness of God within as my total fulfillment is my fulfillment. I am now experiencing total fulfillment.

I am abundance.

I am radiant health.

I am loved and loving.

I am in perfect harmony.

I am totally protected.

I am at perfect peace.

And what I see for myself, I see for all others.

10

THE WORLD HEALING MEDITATION

In 1984 I wrote "The World Healing Meditation" to be used at noon Greenwich time each December 31st beginning in 1986. Over 500 million people participated in that first World Healing Day, and millions continue to join together in this simultaneous global mind-link—not only at the same time each year, but also regularly throughout each month.

The addition of your individual light may be the one to alter the balance in the collective consciousness and achieve the critical mass of spirituality. Come, let us join together in releasing the light of peace, love, forgiveness, and understanding.

In the beginning
In the beginning God

In the beginning God created the heaven and earth.

And God said Let there be light; and there was light.

Now is the time of the new beginning.

I am a co-creator with God, and it is a new heaven that comes as the Good Will of God is expressed on Earth through me.

It is the kingdom of light, love, peace, and understanding.

And I am doing my part to reveal its reality.

I begin with me.

I am a living soul, and the presence of God dwells in me, as me.

I am one with God, and the fullness of the kingdom is mine.

In truth, I am the supreme expression of God.

What is true of me is true of everyone, for God is all and all is God.

I see only the Spirit of God in every soul.

And to every man, woman, and child on Earth, I say:

I love you, for you are me. You are my Holy Self.

I now open my heart, and let the pure essence of unconditional love pour out.

I see it as a Golden Light radiating from the center of my being, and I feel its divine vibration in and through me, above and below me.

I am one with the light.
I am filled with the light.
I am illumined by the light.
I am the light of the world.

With purpose of mind, I send forth the light.

I let the radiance go before me to join the other lights.

I know this is happening all over the world at this moment.

I see the merging lights.

There is now one light. We are the light of the world.

The one light of love, peace, and under-standing is moving.

It flows across the face of the earth, touch-ing and illuminating every one in the shadow of the illusion.

And where there was darkness, there is now the light of Reality.

And the radiance grows, permeating, satu-rating every form of life. There is only the vibra-tion of one perfect life now.
All the kingdoms of the earth respond,
And the planet is alive with light and love.

There is total oneness,
And in this oneness we speak the word.
Let the sense of separation be dissolved.
Let humankind be returned to Godkind.

Let peace come forth in every mind.
Let love flow forth from every heart.
Let forgiveness reign in every soul.
Let understanding be the common bond.

And now from the light of the world, the one Presence and Power of the universe responds.

The activity of God is healing and harmonizing Planet Earth.

Omnipotence is made manifest.

I am seeing the salvation of the planet before my very eyes, as all false beliefs and error patterns are dissolved. The sense of separation is no more; the healing has taken place, and the world is returned to sanity.

This is the beginning of Peace on Earth and Good Will toward all, as love flows forth from every heart, forgiveness reigns in every soul, and all hearts and minds are one in perfect understanding.

It is done. And it is so.

✤ ABOUT THE AUTHOR

John Randolph Price is an internationally known author and lecturer. Formerly a CEO in the corporate world, he has devoted over a quarter of a century to researching the mysteries of ancient wisdom and incorporating those findings into the writing of many books.

In 1981, he and his wife, Jan, formed The Quartus Foundation, a spiritual research and communications organization now headquartered in the Texas hill country.

For information about workshops and the annual Mystery School conducted by John and Jan Price, as well as their monthly publications, please contact:

The Quartus Foundation
P.O. Box 1768
Boerne, TX 78006
(830) 249-3985
(830) 249-3318 (fax)
E-mail: quartus@texas.net
The Quartus Website is:
http://lonestar.texas.net/~quartus

We hope you enjoyed this Hay House book.
If you would like to receive a free
catalog featuring additional Hay House books
and products, or if you would like information
about the Hay Foundation, please contact:

Hay House, Inc.
P.O. Box 5100
Carlsbad, CA 92018-5100

(760) 431-7695 or **(800) 654-5126**
(760) 431-6948 (fax) or **(800) 650-5115 (fax)**

Please visit the Hay House Website at:
www.hayhouse.com